BEAUTIFUL BEASTS

A Collection of Creatures Past and Present

STERLING CHILDREN'S BOOKS
New York

An Imprint of Sterling Publishing
1166 Avenue of the Americas
New York, NY 10036

Written by Camilla de la Bedoyere

STERLING CHILDREN'S BOOKS
and the distinctive Sterling Children's Books logo
are trademarks of Sterling Publishing Co., Inc.

First Sterling edition published in 2015.
Published by Sterling Publishing Co., Inc.

Originally published in 2014 in the United Kingdom by
Marshall Editions
A Quarto Group company
The Old Brewery
6 Blundell Street
London, N7 9BH

© 2014 by Marshall Editions

ISBN 978-1-4549-1459-4

Distributed in Canada by Sterling Publishing
c/o Canadian Manda Group, 664 Annette Street
Toronto, Ontario, Canada M65 2C8

For information about custom editions, special sales, and premium and
corporate purchases, please contact Sterling Special Sales at
800-805-5489 or specialsales@sterlingpublishing.com.

Manufactured in China
Lot #:
2 4 6 8 10 9 7 5 3 1
12/14

www.sterlingpublishing.com/kids

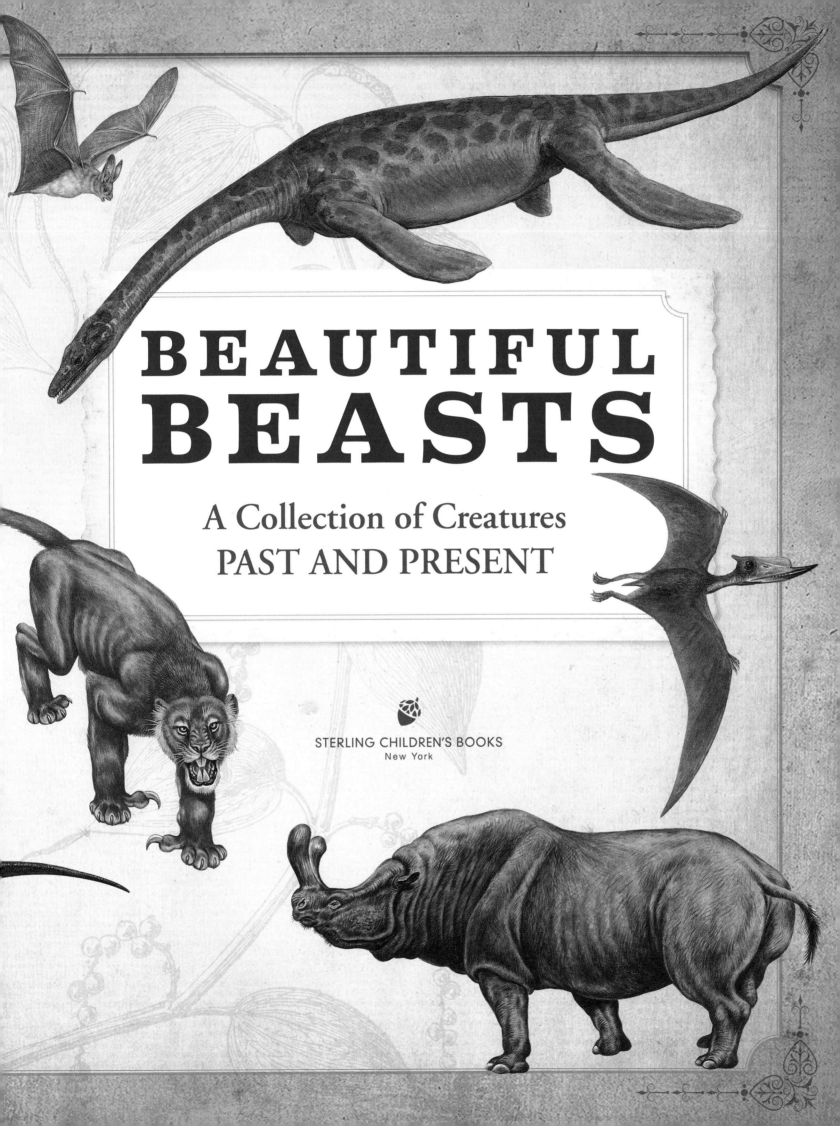

BEAUTIFUL BEASTS

A Collection of Creatures
PAST AND PRESENT

STERLING CHILDREN'S BOOKS
New York

In a time gone by...

From mighty mammoths to terrifying pteranodons, the story of life on Earth is one of beautiful beasts in an ever-changing world.

Once upon a time, the world was a very different place. The animals that lived on prehistoric Earth didn't look like the ones we see in our forests, fields, and oceans today. Massive slithering snakes, hairy rhinos, bone-crunching armored fish, and ferocious dinosaurs ruled the world. In this book, we have collected together a range of extraordinary and beautiful beasts that lived in many different times and places.

FROM TIME TO TIME
The Earth has existed for about 4.6 billion years. At first, it was a burning, exploding, landless, and lifeless place. The story of life began in the oceans, about 3.5 billion years ago. This amazing story is divided into chapters of geological time called eras, periods, and epochs. Dividing time into big chunks makes it easier to understand the way the world has changed and work out when animals and plants lived and died. Each chunk of time is given a name, such as *Jurassic* or *Eocene* and can be put on a timeline from the past to present.

TIMELINE
mya = "millions of years ago"

405 mya – the first wingless insects
380 mya – the first tree-like plants
230 mya – the first dinosaurs
210 mya – the first mamma[l]

ERA

PALEOZOIC **MESO**[ZOIC]

PERIOD/EPOCH

CAMBRIAN	ORDOVICIAN	SILURIAN	DEVONIAN	CARBONIFEROUS	PERMIAN	TRIASSIC	JURAS[SIC]
540 mya	485 mya	445 mya	420 mya	360 mya	300 mya	250 mya	205 mya

470 mya – the first land plants

335 mya – the first amphibians

310 mya – the first reptiles

150 mya – first birds

510 mya – the first fish

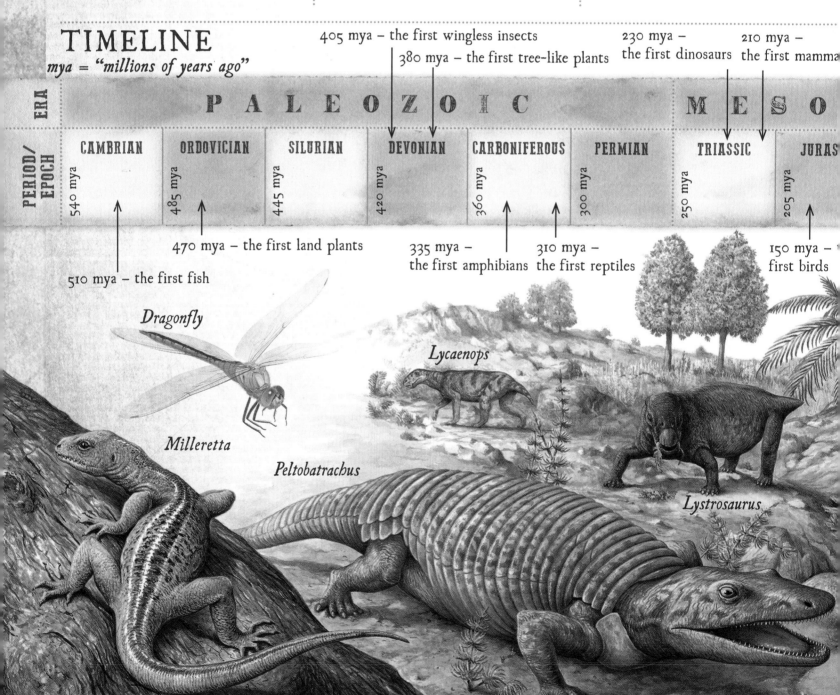

Dragonfly

Milleretta

Peltobatrachus

Lycaenops

Lystrosaurus

ALL THINGS CHANGE

Over millions of years, the world's climate has changed, as have the positions of the continents (large areas of land). During some periods, such as the Cambrian and the Triassic periods, the world was much hotter than it is today. During the Devonian —a time known as the Age of Fish— the sea levels were very high and all the land was clustered around the South Pole. More recently, in the Eocene period, an enormous ice sheet began to spread over the Antarctic.

Ten million years ago the whole world began to cool, and eventually many lands and seas became covered in thick layers of ice and snow.

EXTINCTION

As the world has changed, so have animals and plants. They have to change to survive, and that change is called *evolution*. Those that do not successfully adapt to a new climate or other changing conditions die out. When a type of animal—or plant—dies out forever, it is extinct. Evolution and extinction are normal events in the world's history and have led to the huge variety of incredible living things on Earth.

There have been at least five times in the Earth's history when many animals and plants have died out in a very short time. These are called *mass extinction events* (MEEs). The most famous of all MEEs was the K-T Extinction at the end of the Cretaceous period. The dinosaurs went extinct, but their disappearance meant that mammals could thrive in their place.

200,000 years ago – the first humans: Homo sapiens

Present day

I C	CENOZOIC							
ETACEOUS	PALEOCENE	EOCENE	OLIGOCENE	MIOCENE	PLIOCENE	PLEISTOCENE		HOLOCENE
	65 mya	55 mya	34 mya	24 mya	5 mya	2.5 mya	12,000 years ago	

65 mya – mass extinction event

₃0 mya – the first flowering plants

Robertia

Dicynodon

Procynosuchus

Lycaenops

Animals with Armor

Built like tanks, these armor-plated
beasts appear to be fearless.
Who's tough enough to take a bite?

PANOPLOSAURUS

Late Cretaceous
Pan-OP-lo-SAW-rus

DESMATOSUCHUS

Late Triassic
dez-MAT-oh-SOO-kus

STEGOSAURUS

Late Jurassic
STEG-oh-SAW-rus

COLOSSOCHELYS

Miocene to Pliocene
koh-LOSS-oh-kel-is

**PINK FAIRY
ARMADILLO**

Modern

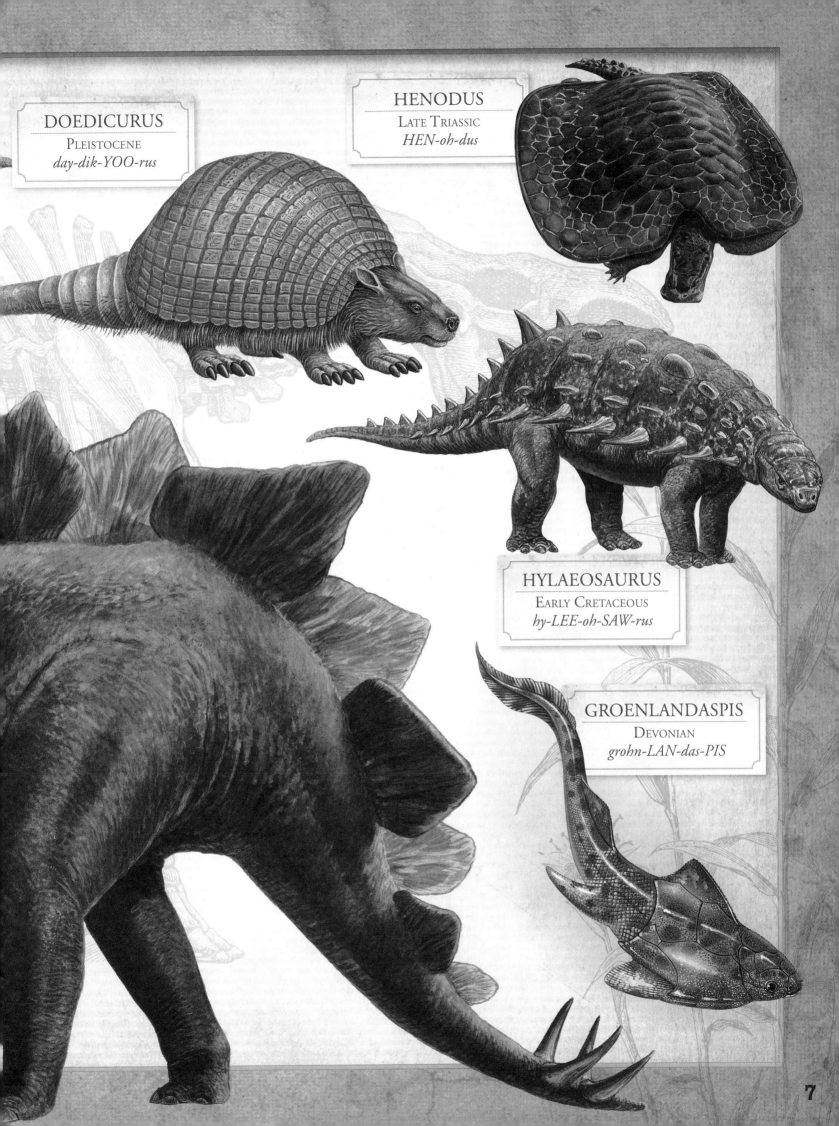

DOEDICURUS
Pleistocene
day-dik-YOO-rus

HENODUS
Late Triassic
HEN-oh-dus

HYLAEOSAURUS
Early Cretaceous
hy-LEE-oh-SAW-rus

GROENLANDASPIS
Devonian
grohn-LAN-das-PIS

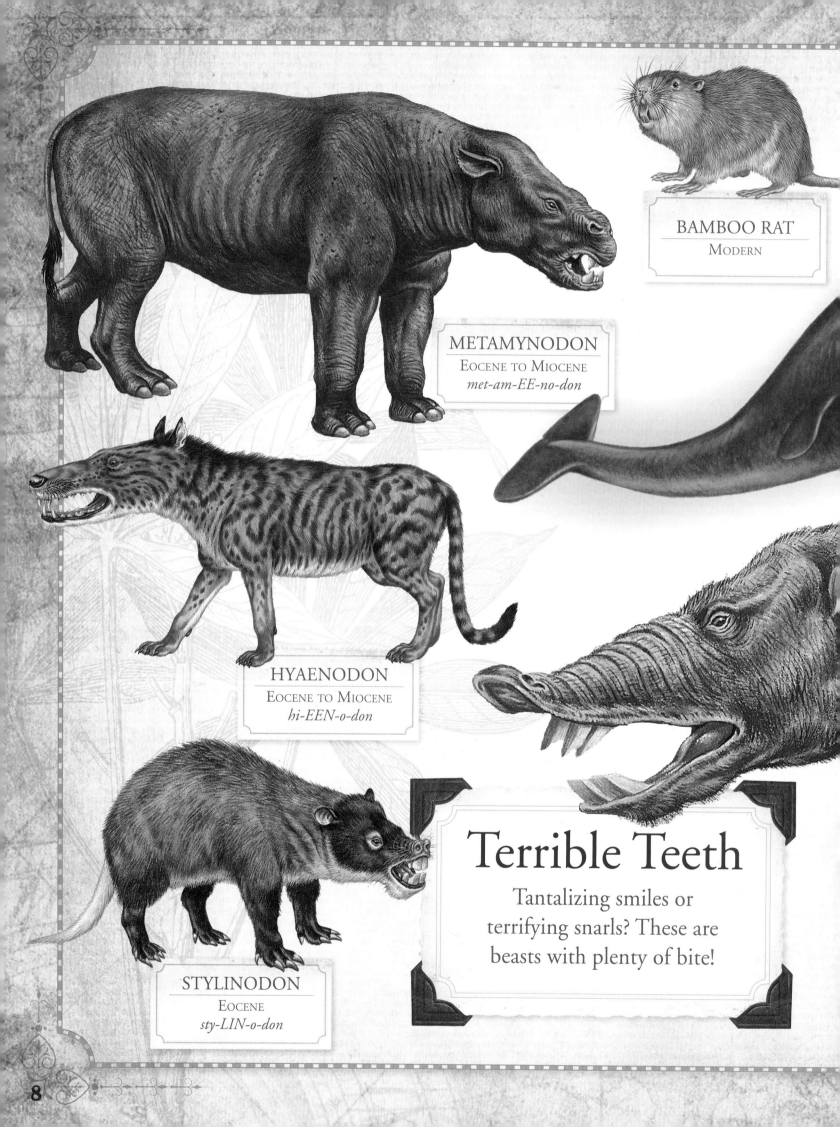

BAMBOO RAT
Modern

METAMYNODON
Eocene to Miocene
met-am-EE-no-don

HYAENODON
Eocene to Miocene
hi-EEN-o-don

STYLINODON
Eocene
sty-LIN-o-don

Terrible Teeth

Tantalizing smiles or terrifying snarls? These are beasts with plenty of bite!

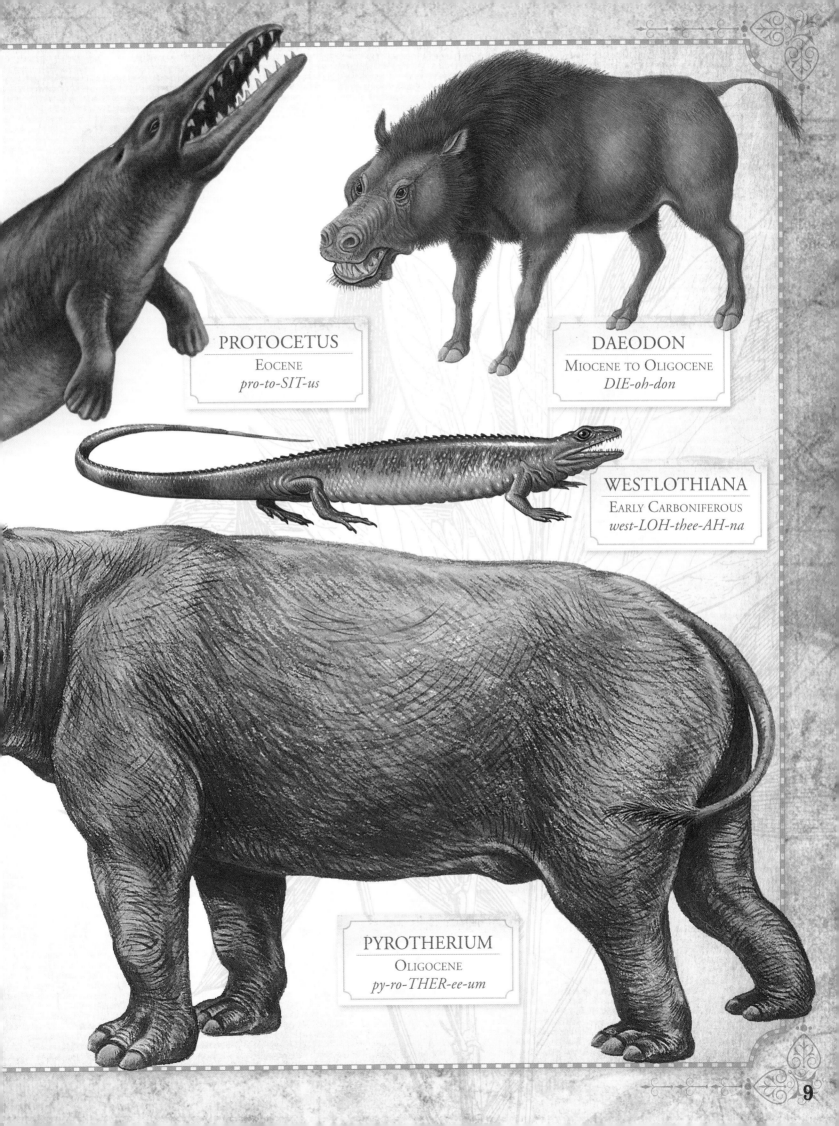

PROTOCETUS
Eocene
pro-to-SIT-us

DAEODON
Miocene to Oligocene
DIE-oh-don

WESTLOTHIANA
Early Carboniferous
west-LOH-thee-AH-na

PYROTHERIUM
Oligocene
py-ro-THER-ee-um

HYRACOTHERIUM
Eocene
hy-rack-o-THER-ee-um

On the Hoof

These fleet-footed animals are related to modern horses, cattle, deer, and camels.

PALAEOTHERIUM
Eocene
pay-lee-oh-THER-ee-um

PRZEWALSKI´S HORSE
Modern

CAMELOPS
Pliocene to Pleistocene
CAM-ell-lops

HIPPIDION
Pleistocene
hip-i-DEE-on

TITANOTYLOPUS
MIOCENE TO PLEISTOCENE
ti-tan-OT-i-LOP-us

ZEBRA
MODERN

MERYCHIPPUS
MIOCENE
MEH-ree-CHIP-us

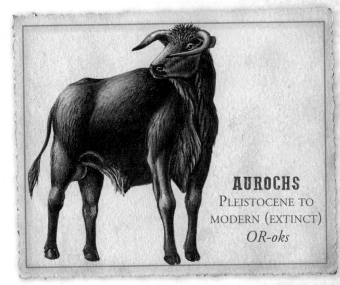

AUROCHS
PLEISTOCENE TO
MODERN (EXTINCT)
OR-oks

POEBROTHERIUM
EOCENE TO OLIGOCENE
POE-ee-bro-THEE-ree-um

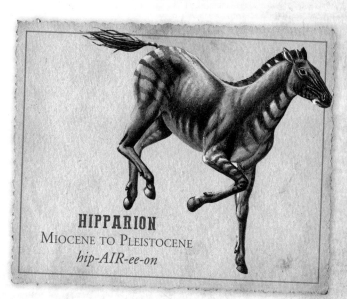

HIPPARION
MIOCENE TO PLEISTOCENE
hip-AIR-ee-on

SIAMOTYRANNUS
Early Cretaceous
sigh-AM-oh-tie-ran-us

KOMODO
DRAGON
Modern

ALBERTOSAURUS
Late Cretaceous
al-bert-oh-SAW-rus

Which of these
ferocious reptiles has
a venomous bite?

ANSWER ON PAGE 64

Terrible Tyrants

Many different reptiles have walked the earth, but dinosaurs were the biggest and scariest. The name *dinosaur* means terrible lizard.

CALLOVOSAURUS
MIDDLE JURASSIC
cal-OH-vo-SAW-rus

ALIORAMUS
LATE CRETACEOUS
al-ee-or-A-mus

TYRANNOSAURUS
LATE CRETACEOUS
ti-RAN-oh-SAW-rus

Speedy Swimmers

Speed is one super survival trick, and swimmers make the most of it.

ASPIDORHYNCHUS
LATE JURASSIC TO EARLY CRETACEOUS
as-PI-dor-RIN-cus

PALAEONISCUM
PERMIAN
PAY-lee-oh-NIS-cum

PERLEIDUS
TRIASSIC
PER-lay-DUS

GREERERPETON
CARBONIFEROUS
GREE-rer-PEH-ton

SAURICHTHYS
TRIASSIC
saw-RIK-this

GOLDFISH

Modern

ENCHODUS

Cretaceous to Eocene

en-KOH-dus

PLATECARPUS

Late Cretaceous

PLAT-ee-CAR-pus

HYPSIDORIS

Eocene

HIP-si-DOR-is

EOBASILEUS
Eocene
eo-bas-il-AY-us

Huge Horns

Used to attack, defend, or attract mates, these horns are beautiful and lifesaving.

ARRHINOCERATOPS
Late Cretaceous
ay-rine-oh-SERRA-tops

MONTANOCERATOPS
Late Cretaceous
mon-TAN-oh-ser-a-tops

ELASMOTHERIUM
Pliocene to Pleistocene
el-AS-mo-THER-ee-um

JACKSON'S
CHAMELEON
Modern

AFRICAN
BUFFALO
Modern

CENTROSAURUS
Late Cretaceous
cen-TROH-SAW-rus

EMBOLOTHERIUM
Eocene
EM-bol-o-THER-ee-um

17

Peculiar Birds

Strange beaks and fabulous feathers could not protect most of these birds from extinction.

OSTEODONTORNIS

Miocene
OST-ee-oh-don-TORN-is

ARCHAEOPTERYX

Late Jurassic to
Early Cretaceous
ark-ee-OP-ter-iks

HELMETED HORNBILL

Modern

DIATRYMA

Eocene
Die-ah-tree-ma

DODO

Modern (extinct)

PLATE-BILLED MOUNTAIN TOUCAN
MODERN

GREAT AUK
MODERN (EXTINCT)

Two of these birds had teeth! Can you spot which ones?

ANSWER ON PAGE 64

GIANT MOA
MODERN (EXTINCT)

ARGENTAVIS
MIOCENE
ar-jen-TAY-vis

PACHYCEPHALOSAURUS
Late Cretaceous
PAK-ee-SEF-a-loh-SAW-rus

ACANTHOSTEGA
Devonian
ah-CAN-thoh-STAY-ga

ANATOSAURUS
Late Cretaceous
an-at-oh-SAW-rus

DILOPHOSAURUS
Early Jurassic
die-LOAF-oh-SAW-rus

Funny Faces

Beauty is in the eye of the
beholder. Some beasts have a face
only a mother could love.

PROBOSCIS
MONKEY

Modern

CRASSIGYRINUS

Carboniferous

KRA-sig-i-RIN-us

GERROTHORAX

Late Triassic

GEH-roh-THOR-ax

TSINTAOSAURUS

Late Cretaceous

JING-dow-SAW-rus

MIACIS
PALEOCENE TO EOCENE
my-AH-sis

CRUSAFONTIA
EARLY CRETACEOUS
croos-a-FONT-ee-a

MEGAZOSTRODON
LATE TRIASSIC TO EARLY JURASSIC
meg-a-ZOST-roh-don

EUROPEAN RABBIT
MODERN

Mini Mammals

The first mammals lived about 200 million years ago. They were small and furry.

NECROLESTES
MIOCENE
nec-ro-LES-tes

HARAMIYA
Late Triassic to Early Jurassic
har-a-MEE-ya

ZALAMBDALESTES
Late Cretaceous
zal-am-dal-EST-es

PTILODUS
Paleocene
til-oh-dus

ALPHADON
Late Cretaceous to Eocene
ALF-a-don

PURGATORIUS
Paleocene
purg-a-TOR-ee-us

METACHEIROMYS
Eocene
meta-KIR-oh-mis

DORYASPIS
DEVONIAN
dor-ee-ASP-is

LAMBEOSAURUS
LATE CRETACEOUS
LAM-bee-oh-SAW-rus

THORNY DEVIL
MODERN

SYNTHETOCERAS
MIOCENE
sin-thet-oh-SER-as

SPINY TAILED SKINK
Modern

SCLERORHYNCHUS
Late Cretaceous
skleh-roh-RIN-kuss

ELGINIA
Permian
el-GIN-ee-ah

Strange Spikes
These bony bits, hard horns, and super-large scales and spikes are not just for decoration.

STYRACOSAURUS
Early Cretaceous
sty-RAK-oh-SAW-rus

PROGANOCHELYS
Late Triassic
pro-gan-oh-KEEL-is

ANUROGNATHUS
Late Jurassic
ann-yew-ro-KNAY-thus

ICARONYCTERIS
Eocene
ik-a-roh-NIK-ter-is

Masters of the Air

See these aerial acrobats swoop, soar, glide, flit, and flap through the skies.

GREAT
BLACK-BACKED
GULL
Modern

DIMORPHODON
Early Jurassic
dy-MORF-oh-don

QUETZALCOATLUS

Late Cretaceous
ket-zal-coh-at-lus

KUEHNEOSAURUS

Late Triassic
kew-nee-oh-SAW-rus

PTERANODON

Late Cretaceous
teh-RAN-oh-don

RHAMPHORHYNCHUS

Late Jurassic
RAM-for-INK-us

Which of these
fluffy fliers was an
ancient type of bat?

ANSWER ON PAGE 64

DSUNGARIPTERUS

Early Cretaceous
SUNG-a-RIPT-er-us

SCAPHOGNATHUS

Late Jurassic
skaf-oh-KNAY-thus

DIMETRODON
PERMIAN
di-MEE-troh-don

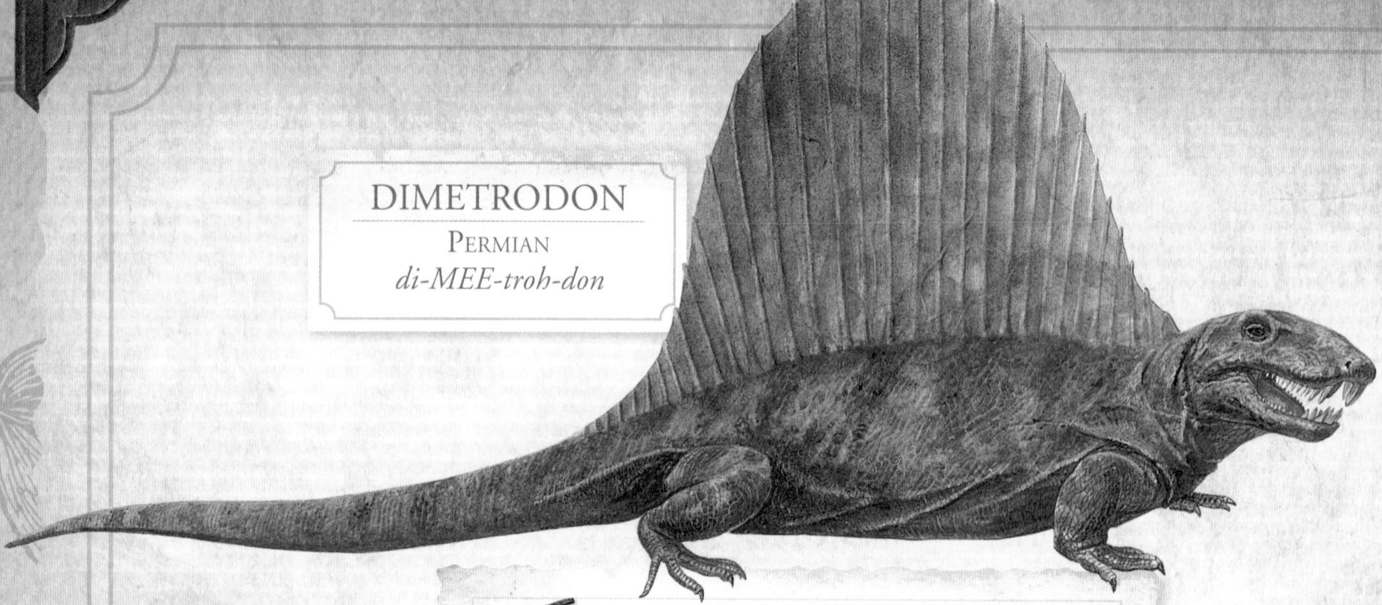

Bizarre Bodies

Animals, from prehistory to today, come in many shapes and sizes. It takes all sorts!

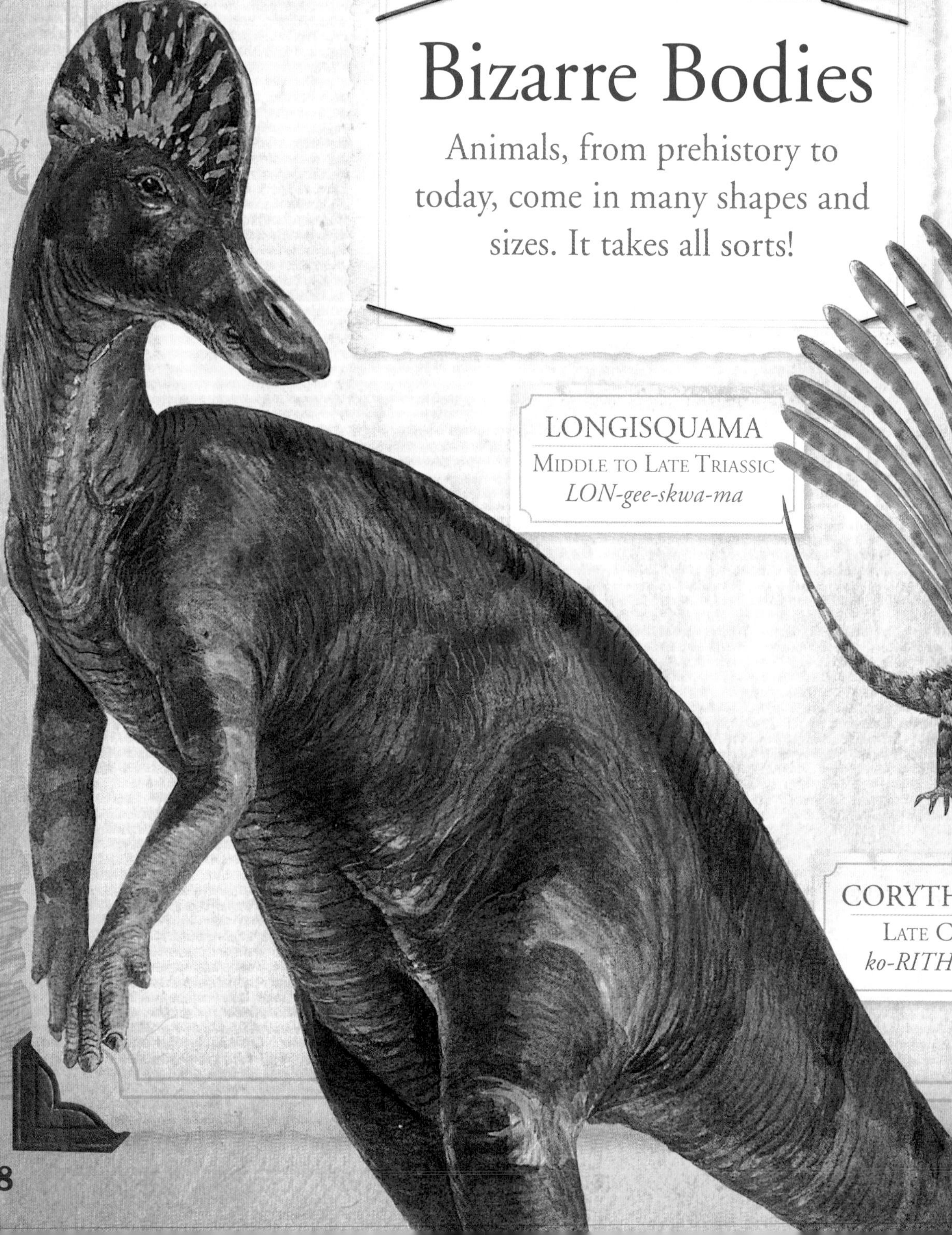

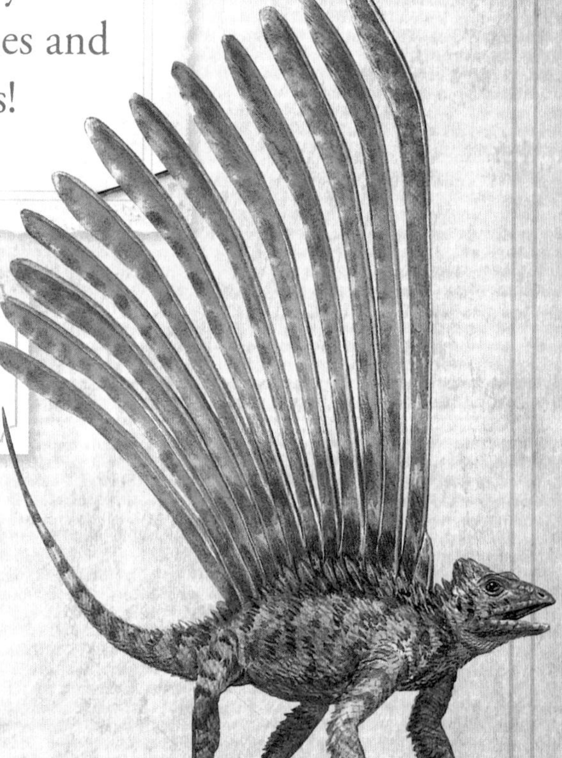

LONGISQUAMA
MIDDLE TO LATE TRIASSIC
LON-gee-skwa-ma

CORYTHOSAURUS
LATE CRETACEOUS
ko-RITH-oh-SAW-rus

Which of these creatures used its strange shape to keep warm?

ANSWER ON PAGE 64

DIPLOCAULUS
Permian
dip-lo-KAW-lus

OURANOSAURUS
Cretaceous
OO-ran-oh-SAW-rus

EOMANIS
Eocene
eo-MAN-is

FRILLED LIZARD
Modern

PARASAUROLOPHUS
Late Cretaceous
PARA-saw-ROL-oh-fus

JAGUAR
Modern

COELURUS
Late Jurassic to Early Cretaceous
SEE-loo-rus

PLANOCEPHALOSAURUS
Late Triassic
PLANE-oh-SEF-al-oh-SAW-rus

TERRESTRISUCHUS
Late Triassic
ter-EST-ri-SOOK-us

HAPALOPS
Miocene
HAP-al-ops

Spots and Speckles

These beauties are gorgeous in their coats, scales, and skins of many colors.

BOROPHAGUS
MIOCENE TO PLIOCENE
bo-RO-fay-gus

PLANETETHERIUM
PALEOCENE
PLAN-et-ee-THER-ee-um

GEMUENDINA
DEVONIAN
JEM-oo-en-DEE-na

NORTHERN LEOPARD FROG
MODERN

COELUROSAURAVUS
Permian ·
see-lur-OH-saw-AY-vus

HYPSILOPHODON
Early Cretaceous
hip-sil-OH-fo-don

VELOCIRAPTOR
Late Cretaceous
vel-O-si-RAP-tor

Can you spot which
of these creatures
traveled by gliding?

ANSWER ON PAGE 64

LIOPLEURODON
Middle to Late Jurassic
LIE-oh-PLER-oh-don

MOSASAURUS
Late Cretaceous
moh-za-SAW-rus

THOATHERIUM
Miocene
tho-ath-ER-ee-um

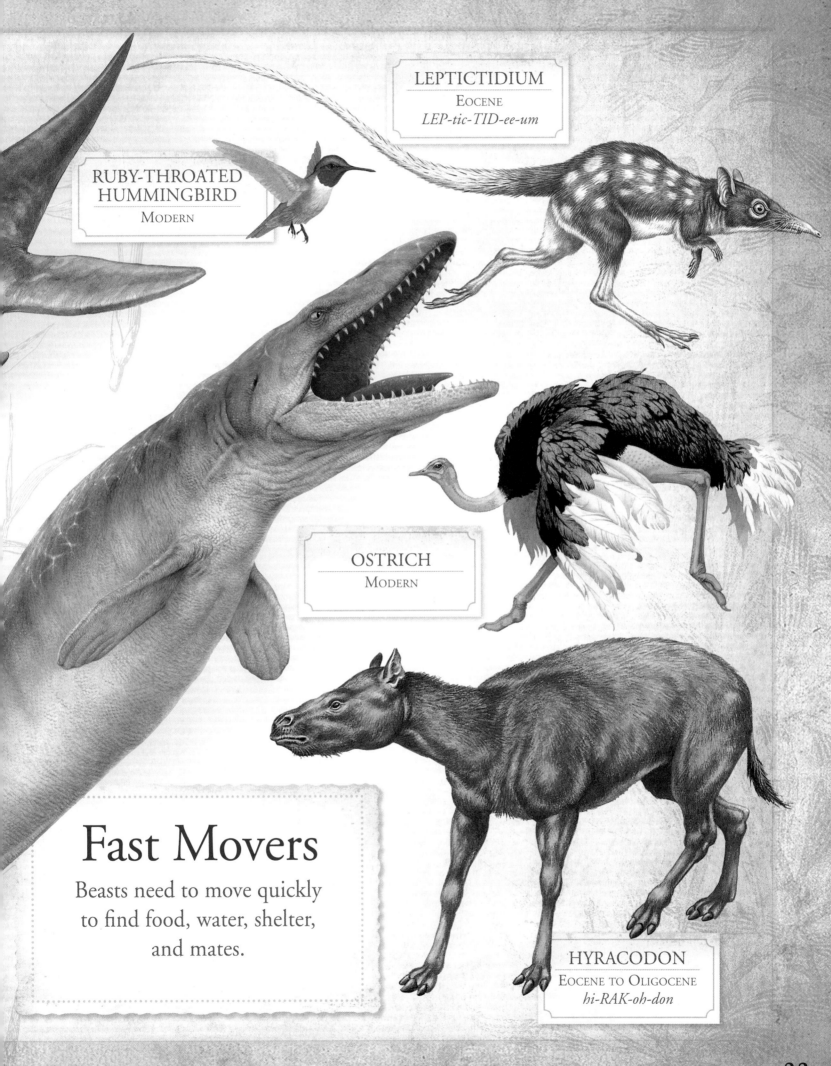

RUBY-THROATED
HUMMINGBIRD
MODERN

LEPTICTIDIUM
EOCENE
LEP-tic-TID-ee-um

OSTRICH
MODERN

Fast Movers

Beasts need to move quickly to find food, water, shelter, and mates.

HYRACODON
EOCENE TO OLIGOCENE
hi-RAK-oh-don

ECHINODON
Early Cretaceous
eh-KY-no-don

ORNITHOSUCHUS
Late Triassic
OR-nith-oh-SOOK-us

GREAT JERBOA
Modern

Two Feet

Because of the shape of their hip bones, some beasts walk on four legs while others just use two.

PRENOCEPHALE
Late Cretaceous
pren-oh-SEF-a-lee

HETERODONTOSAURUS

Early Jurassic

HET-er-oh-DONT-oh-SAW-rus

MASSOSPONDYLUS

Late Triassic to Early Jurassic

MASS-oh-SPOND-i-lus

EUPARKERIA

Early Triassic

YOO-park-EE-ree-a

SINOSAUROPTERYX

Early Cretaceous

SIGH-no-saw-OP-ter-iks

PROCOPTODON

Pleistocene

pro-COP-toh-don

Mighty Mammoths

The most magnificent of all mammals, these are members of the elephant family.

DEINOTHERIUM
Miocene to Early Pleistocene
dine-o-THER-ee-um

ASTRAPOTHERIUM
Oligocene to Miocene
ast-rap-oh-THER-ee-um

MAMMUTHUS MERIDIONALIS
Pleistocene
ma-mu-thus mer-id-ee-on-AL-is

ASIAN ELEPHANT
MODERN

Which of these
giants lived in the
coldest places?
ANSWER ON PAGE 64

WOOLLY MAMMOTH
PLEISTOCENE TO MODERN (EXTINCT)

AMEBELODON
MIOCENE
am-eh-BEL-oh-don

Nibblers and Grazers

It takes strong jaws and tough teeth to munch through grass, seeds, and nuts.

ARIZONA COTTON RAT
Modern

OLIGOKYPHUS
Triassic to Jurassic
OL-ig-oh-KY-fus

BLASTOMERYX
Oligocene to Miocene
blast-OM-er-ix

PACHYRUKHOS
Oligocene to Miocene
pa-kee-ROO-kos

ARGYROLAGUS
Pliocene
ar-ger-oh-LA-gus

PROTYPOTHERIUM
MIOCENE
PRO-tip-o-THER-ee-um

AFRICAN WILD ASS
MODERN

RHYNCHIPPUS
EOCENE TO
OLIGOCENE
rin-kip-us

EOCARDIA
MIOCENE
ee-oh-CARD-ee-a

CERATOGAULUS
MIOCENE TO PLIOCENE
SER-at-oh-GOW-lus

PALAEOLAGUS
EOCENE TO OLIGOCENE
pay-lee-oh-LA-gus

PLEUROSAURUS
Late Jurassic
PLOO-roh-SAW-rus

PROTARCHAEOPTERYX
Early Cretaceous
pro-TARK-ee-OP-ter-iks

EUOPLOCEPHALUS
Late Cretaceous
you-op-loh-SEF-ah-lus

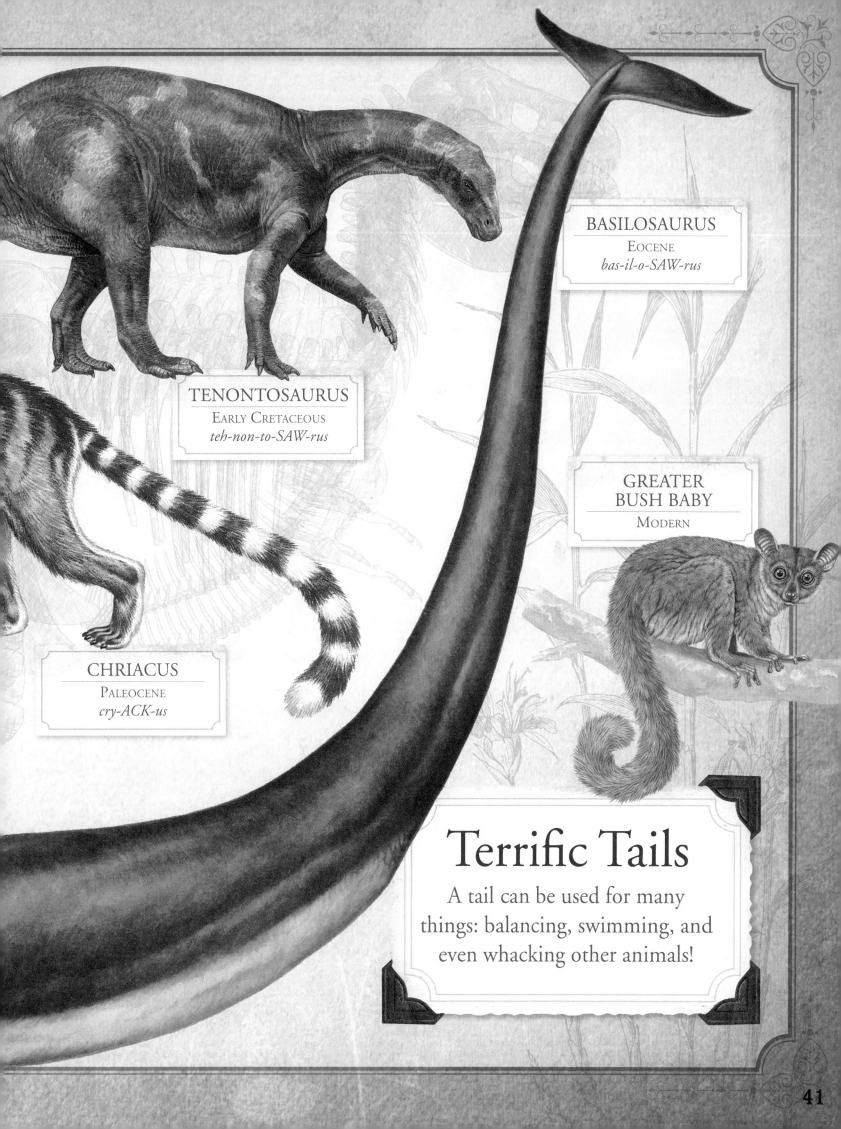

BASILOSAURUS
EOCENE
bas-il-o-SAW-rus

TENONTOSAURUS
EARLY CRETACEOUS
teh-non-to-SAW-rus

**GREATER
BUSH BABY**
MODERN

CHRIACUS
PALEOCENE
cry-ACK-us

Terrific Tails

A tail can be used for many
things: balancing, swimming, and
even whacking other animals!

Incredible Hulks

When size is on your side
there is little to fear.
Big is beautiful!

HIPPOPOTAMUS

MODERN

BARAPASAURUS

EARLY JURASSIC
ba-RA-pa-SAW-rus

RIOJASAURUS

Late Triassic

ree-okah-SAW-rus

BRACHIOSAURUS

Late Jurassic

BRACK-ee-oh-SAW-rus

PLATEOSAURUS

Late Triassic

PLAT-ee-oh-SAW-rus

ARSINOITHERIUM

Eocene to Oligocene

ars-in-oy-THER-ee-um

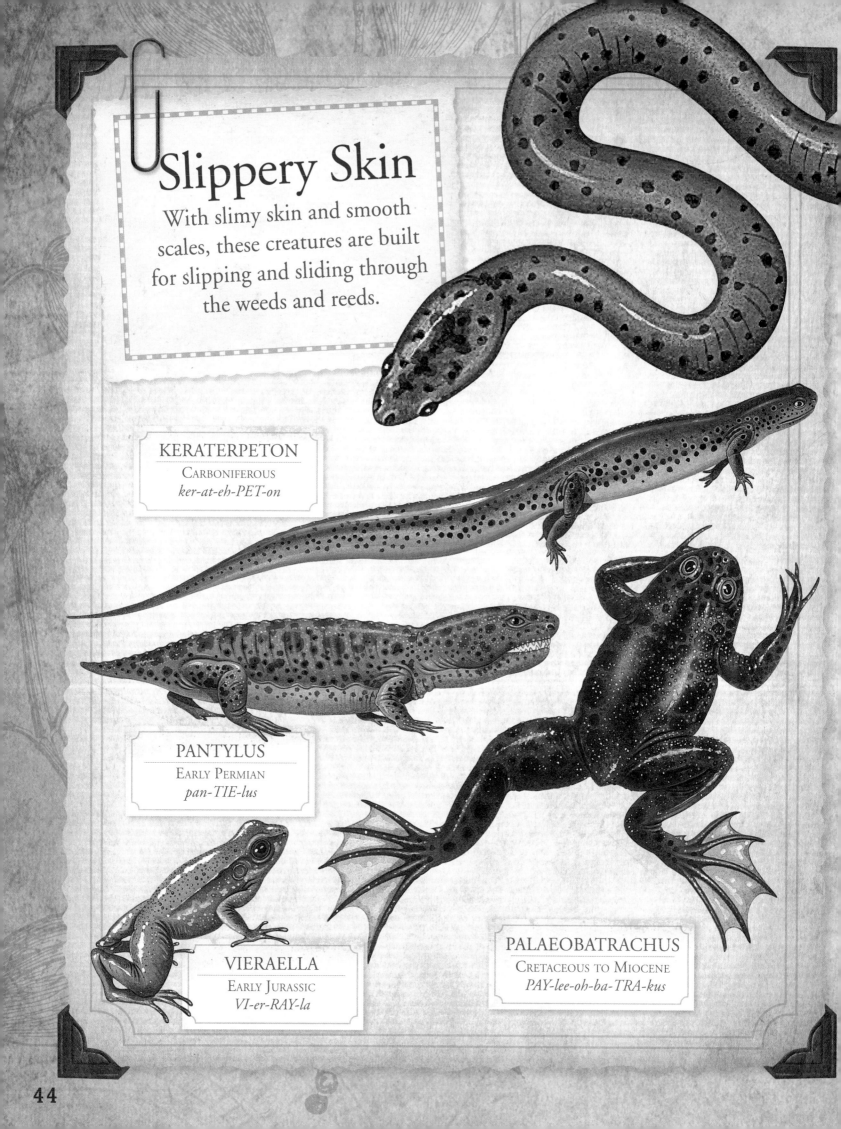

Slippery Skin

With slimy skin and smooth scales, these creatures are built for slipping and sliding through the weeds and reeds.

KERATERPETON
Carboniferous
ker-at-eh-PET-on

PANTYLUS
Early Permian
pan-TIE-lus

VIERAELLA
Early Jurassic
VI-er-RAY-la

PALAEOBATRACHUS
Cretaceous to Miocene
PAY-lee-oh-ba-TRA-kus

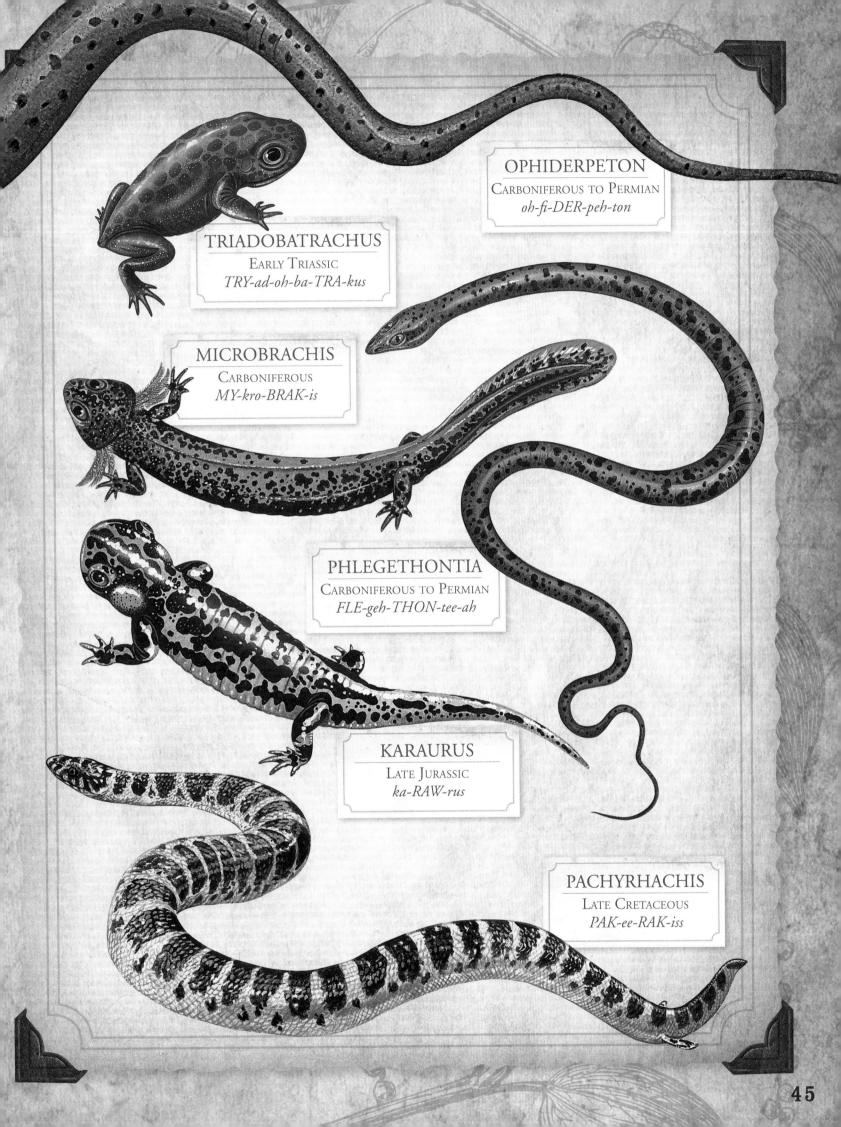

OPHIDERPETON
Carboniferous to Permian
oh-fi-DER-peh-ton

TRIADOBATRACHUS
Early Triassic
TRY-ad-oh-ba-TRA-kus

MICROBRACHIS
Carboniferous
MY-kro-BRAK-is

PHLEGETHONTIA
Carboniferous to Permian
FLE-geh-THON-tee-ah

KARAURUS
Late Jurassic
ka-RAW-rus

PACHYRHACHIS
Late Cretaceous
PAK-ee-RAK-iss

ARCHAEOTHERIUM

Eocene to Oligocene
ARK-ee-oh-THER-ee-um

COELOPHYSIS

Triassic to Jurassic
seel-oh-FY-sis

ORNITHOMIMUS

Late Cretaceous
ORN-ith-oh-MIM-us

Can you tell which
of these beasts were
hunters?

ANSWER ON PAGE 64

DIACODEXIS

Eocene
dee-a-co-DEX-is

COBELODUS
Permian
COB-e-LOH-dus

Super Stripes
In the right environment, stylish stripes can help you hide.

CLADOSICTIS
Late Oligocene to Early Miocene
CLAY-doh-sik-tis

INDIAN STRIPED PALM SQUIRREL
Modern

HYPACROSAURUS
Late Cretaceous
hi-PAK-ro-SAW-rus

PLESIOSAURUS
Late Jurassic
PLEEZ-ee-oh-SAW-rus

SMOOTH
HAMMERHEAD
Modern

PIRANHA
Modern

MACROPLATA
Early Jurassic
mac-roh-PLAT-a

48

ELASMOSAURUS
LATE CRETACEOUS
el-az-mo-SAW-rus

MESOSAURUS
PERMIAN
MES-oh-SAW-rus

Danger Below

Underneath the rippling surface of the water, danger lurks in the form of these hungry hunters.

ICHTHYOSAURUS
LATE TRIASSIC TO JURASSIC
IK-thee-oh-SAW-rus

SHONISAURUS
LATE TRIASSIC
SHOH-nee-SAW-rus

PLESICTIS
Oligocene to Miocene
ples-IK-tis

CHAPALMALANIA
Pliocene
CHAP-al-mal-AN-ee-a

TOXODON
Miocene to Pleistocene
TOX-o-don

PHLAOCYON
Oligocene to Miocene
phlay-oh-SIGH-on

NOTOSTYLOPS
Eocene
NOT-o-STY-lops

DESMOSTYLUS
Ogliocene to Miocene
des-mos-STIL-us

CERDOCYON AVIUS
Pliocene
ker-do-SIGH-on

ICTITHERIUM
Miocene to Early Pliocene
IC-tee-THER-ee-um

MEGATHERIUM
Pleistocene to Holocene
Meg-a-THER-ee-um

Cute and cuddly

These critters might be soft and furry, but you wouldn't want to give one a hug.

SPECTACLED
CAIMAN
MODERN

Lots of Crocs

Today's crocodiles look like
their ancient relatives, but some of
these beasts ate plants!

TELEOSAURUS
MIDDLE JURASSIC
TELL-ee-oh-SAW-rus

TERRESTRISUCHUS
LATE TRIASSIC
ter-EST-ri-SOOK-us

PROTOSUCHUS
EARLY JURASSIC
PROE-toh-SOOK-us

METRIORHYNCHUS
Middle Jurassic to Early Cretaceous
MET-ree-oh-RINK-us

BERNISSARTIA
Early Cretaceous
BER-nih-SART-ee-ah

DEINOSUCHUS
Cretaceous to Pliocene
DINE-oh-SOOK-us

MEGALOCEROS
PLIOCENE TO RECENT
meg-al-oh-SER-os

Awesome Antlers

Antlers and horns contain bone. They make great weapons for fighting enemies and other males.

MOOSE
MODERN

ILINGOCEROS
MIOCENE
ill-in-go-SER-os

PROLIBYTHERIUM
MIOCENE
pro-lib-i-THER-ee-um

SIVATHERIUM
MIOCENE TO
MODERN (EXTINCT)
si-va-THER-ee-um

RED DEER
MODERN

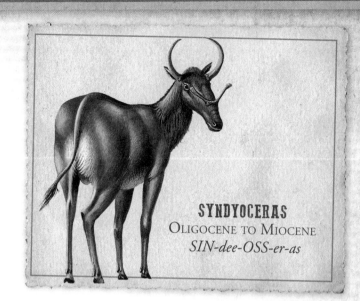

SYNDYOCERAS
OLIGOCENE TO MIOCENE
SIN-dee-OSS-er-as

HAYOCEROS
RECENT
hay-oh-SER-os

GREATER KUDU
MODERN

PELOROVIS
PLIOCENE TO RECENT
pel-oh-ROH-vis

EUCLADOCEROS
PLIOCENE TO MODERN (EXTINCT)
yu-clad-o-SER-os

Extraordinary Necks

Long, strong, and bendy necks—very useful for looking around corners (and reaching treetops).

GIRAFFE
MODERN

GIRAFFE WEEVIL
MODERN

CERESIOSAURUS
EARLY TRIASSIC
seh-REEZ-ee-oh-SAW-rus

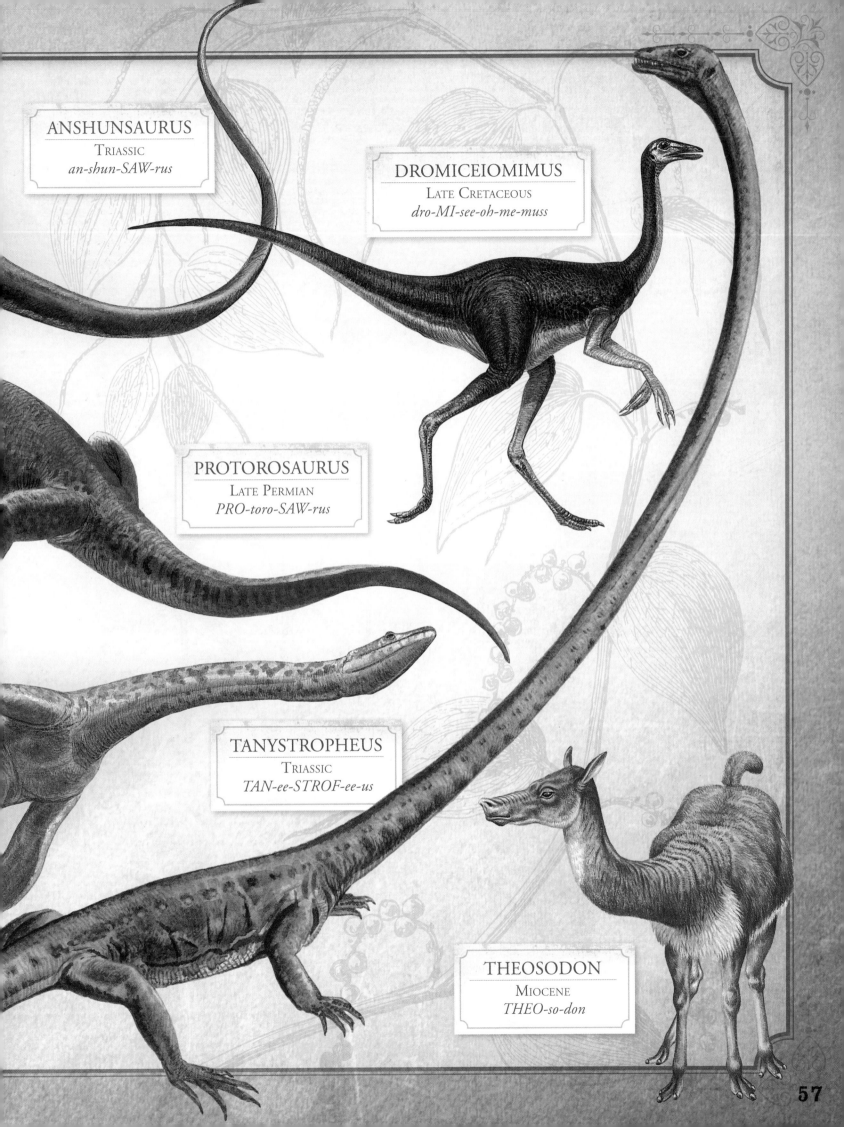

ANSHUNSAURUS
Triassic
an-shun-SAW-rus

DROMICEIOMIMUS
Late Cretaceous
dro-MI-see-oh-me-muss

PROTOROSAURUS
Late Permian
PRO-toro-SAW-rus

TANYSTROPHEUS
Triassic
TAN-ee-STROF-ee-us

THEOSODON
Miocene
THEO-so-don

SMILODON

PEISTOCENE TO
EARLY HOLOCENE
SMY-loh-don

Perfect Pet?

From the past to the present,
there have been many fierce
cat- and doglike creatures.

DOMESTIC DOG

MODERN

DINOFELIS

PLIOCENE TO PLEISTOCENE
die-no-FEE-lis

CAVE LION

PLEISTOCENE

EUSMILUS

Eocene to Oligocene
yoo-SMY-lus

Can you tell which of
these beasts are dogs
and which are cats?

ANSWER ON PAGE 64

MEGANTEREON

Pliocene to Pleistocene
meg-an-TER-ee-on

PACHYCROCUTA

Pliocene to Pleistocene
pa-kee-croh-KEW-ta

HESPEROCYON

Eocene to Oligocene
hes-per-oh-SY-on

COLOCOLO

Modern

HEMICYON

Miocene
hem-EE-sy-on

PTERASPIS
Devonian
ter-AP-sis

CLADOSELACHE
Devonian
clad-OH-sel-ACK

PLAICE
Modern

PHARYNGOLEPIS
Silurian
far-IN-gol-EP-is

JAMOYTIUS
Silurian
ja-MOY-tee-us

SCAPANORHYNCHUS
Cretaceous
sca-PAN-or-INK-us

SPATHOBATIS
Jurassic to Cretaceous
SPA-tho-BAT-is

ENCHODUS
CRETACEOUS TO PALEOCENE
en-KOH-dus

STETHACANTHUS
CARBONIFEROUS
STETH-a-CAN-thus

PLATYSOMUS
CARBONIFEROUS TO TRIASSIC
PLA-tis-OH-mus

DREPANASPIS
DEVONIAN
dre-pa-NAS-pis

Fabulous Fish

From small fry to tyrants,
fish have ruled the seas for more
than 400 million years.

DIPNORHYNCHUS
DEVONIAN
DIP-nor-RIN-kus

Nice Noses

A collection of snouts, muzzles, proboscises, and noses. Pick your favorite!

PTERODAUSTRO

Early Cretaceous
TER-oh-DOW-stro

RYTIODUS

Miocene
RYE-tee-OH-dus

MOERITHERIUM

Eocene to Oligocene
moh-er-ee-THER-ee-um

STENEOFIBER

Eocene to Pliocene
STEN-ee-o-FIB-er

METRIDIOCHOERUS

Pliocene to Pleistocene
me-TRID-ee-oh-ko-AIR-us

KANNEMEYERIA

EARLY TRIASSIC
KAN-eh-MAY-er-ee-a

MACRAUCHENIA

MIOCENE TO MODERN (EXTINCT)
mac-row-KEEN-ee-a

CERATOSAURUS

LATE JURASSIC
ser-at-oh-SAW-rus

NORTHERN PIKA

MODERN

ANSWERS

ICARONYCTERIS

MASTERS OF THE AIR

Q: Which of these fluffy fliers was an ancient type of bat?

A: Icaronycteris—it was one of the earliest known bats and was very similar to modern bats.

PECULIAR BIRDS

Q: Two of these birds had teeth! Can you spot which ones?

A: Osteodontornis and Archaeopteryx

OSTEODONTORNIS

TERRIBLE TYRANTS

Q: Which of these ferocious reptiles has a venomous bite?

A: The Komodo dragon—scientists haven't found evidence that any dinosaurs were venomous.

FAST MOVERS

Q: Can you spot which of these creatures traveled by gliding?

A: Coelurosauravus—scientists think this small reptile glided between tree branches.

DIMETRODON

BIZARRE BODIES

Q: Which of these creatures used its strange shape to keep warm?

A: Dimetrodon—the large sail on its back would warm up in the sun, and from there, warmed blood would be carried around the rest of its body.

MIGHTY MAMMOTHS

Q: Which of these giants lived in the coldest places?

A: The woolly mammoth—it had a thick covering of hair to keep warm during the Ice Age.

COBELODUS

INDIAN STRIPED
PALM SQUIRREL

SUPER STRIPES

Q: Can you tell which of these beasts were hunters?

A: Cobelodus ate crustaceans and squid. Coelophysis ate small reptiles and the ancestors of mammals. Ornithomimus probably ate insects and small animals, as well as fruit and leaves.

PERFECT PET?

Q: Can you tell which of these beasts are dogs and which are cats?

A: Smilodon, Eusmilus, Megantereon, Dinofelis, Colocolo, and the cave lion are all related to cats. The domestic dog and Hesperocyon are both part of the dog family.

HESPEROCYON

64